The ANT
GRASSHOPPER

THE CAST

ANT

GRASSHOPPER

PARROT

COBRA

MONGOOSE

TIGER

GRASSHOPPER: Hello, Ant.

ANT: Hello, Grasshopper.

GRASSHOPPER: You and I are the smallest creatures in the jungle, so we should be friends.

ANT: Okay, Grasshopper. That's a good idea.

GRASSHOPPER: Let's play a game together, Ant. Let's see how far we can jump.

ANT: I'm not sure . . .

GRASSHOPPER: Come on, it's easy. Just watch me!

(Grasshopper jumps over the river.)

4

ANT: Well, if you think so . . .

(Ant jumps, but lands on a rock in the middle of the river.)

Help, Grasshopper! Help me!
Go and get a rope!

GRASSHOPPER: Don't worry, Ant!
I'll get a rope and be back
as soon as I can!

5

PARROT: Why are you looking so worried, Grasshopper?

GRASSHOPPER: Ant is stuck on a rock in the middle of the river. I need some rope to rescue him.

PARROT: Hmmm . . . I think I can help you. I haven't any rope, but I can get you some vine. But first you must help me.

GRASSHOPPER: I will help you
if I can. What do you want?

PARROT: I want some bananas to eat,
but Cobra is guarding the tree.
If you get me some bananas,
I will get you some vine.

GRASSHOPPER: I will ask
Cobra to move!

COBRA: Why are you looking so worried, Grasshopper?

GRASSHOPPER: Ant is stuck on a rock in the middle of the river. I can rescue him if you leave the banana tree. Then Parrot can get some bananas, and I can get some vine. Then I can rescue Ant.

COBRA: Hmmm . . . I think I can help you. But first you must help me.

GRASSHOPPER: I will help you
if I can. What do you want?

 COBRA: I want some water,
but Mongoose is guarding the well.
If Mongoose leaves the well
so that I can get some water,
I will leave the banana tree.

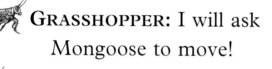 **GRASSHOPPER:** I will ask
Mongoose to move!

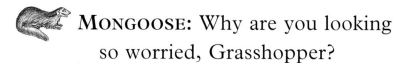 **MONGOOSE:** Why are you looking so worried, Grasshopper?

 **GRASSHOPPER:** Ant is stuck on a rock in the middle of the river. I can rescue him if you leave the well. Then Cobra can get some water, and Parrot can get some bananas, and I can get some vine. Then I can rescue Ant.

MONGOOSE: Hmmm . . . I think I can help you. But first you must help me.

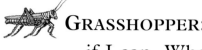 **GRASSHOPPER:** I will help you if I can. What do you want?

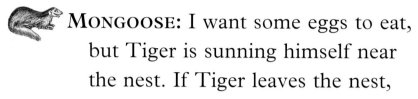 **MONGOOSE:** I want some eggs to eat, but Tiger is sunning himself near the nest. If Tiger leaves the nest, I will leave the well.

GRASSHOPPER: I will ask Tiger to move!

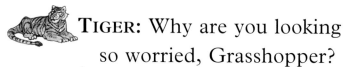

TIGER: Why are you looking so worried, Grasshopper?

GRASSHOPPER: It's a long story! Ant is stuck on a rock in the middle of the river. I can rescue him if you leave the nest and go somewhere else to sun yourself. Will you please help me?

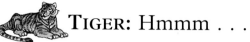 **TIGER:** Hmmm . . .
The sun is starting to go down,
and my tail is already in shadow.
Yes, I will leave the nest.

 **MONGOOSE:** Good! Now I will
leave the well.

COBRA: Good! Now I will leave the banana tree.

PARROT: Good! Now I will give you some vine, Grasshopper.

GRASSHOPPER: Good! Now I can rescue Ant! *(He quickly throws the vine to Ant.)*

ANT: Thank you, Grasshopper.
I'm glad to be off that rock,
but next time, don't take so long!